W9-DFZ-247

DREAM BIG JOURNAL

Weekly Wake-ups to Help You Reach
Your Most Ambitious Goals

BOB GOFF

NELSON
BOOKS

An Imprint of Thomas Nelson

Dream Big Journal

© 2021 Bob Goff

Published in Nashville, Tennessee, by Nelson Books, an imprint of Thomas Nelson. Nelson Books and Thomas Nelson are registered trademarks of HarperCollins Christian Publishing, Inc.

Represented by Alive Literary Agency, www.aliveliterary.com.

Thomas Nelson titles may be purchased in bulk for educational, business, fundraising, or sales promotional use. For information, please e-mail SpecialMarkets@ThomasNelson.com.

With thanks to Carrie Marrs for her help pulling this together.

ISBN 978-1-4002-3060-0

Printed in the United States of America

21 22 23 24 25 LSC 10 9 8 7 6 5 4 3 2 1

CONTENTS

CONTENTS

INTRODUCTION

Welcome! You made it to the *Dream Big Journal*— your launching pad for new stuff! I'm glad you're meeting up with me here.

You're here because you've got a lot of dreams in you. Maybe they haven't taken any shape yet; they're just a big blob of ideas. Maybe you haven't even discovered them yet. That's okay. The beginnings of them are inside of you. You're bursting with possibilities, gifts, and abilities that only you—the once-ever-in-history you—can offer. Jesus invited you on this adventure called your life, and He did it so you could be fully alive and fully His and fulfill the ambitions He made you to have.

You're here because you want to become awake to those ambitions by becoming awake to yourself and your God-given purposes. You want to release amazing things into the world and are willing to do whatever it takes to make it happen. I'm really excited you're going to figure out what's next for you.

Setting aside time for personal reflection about who you are, why you think what you think, and why you do what you do is the heavy lifting you need to do if you want to accomplish things in your life you haven't been able to yet. Working through this journal will help you discover your most worthwhile ambition and keep moving toward it. Think of this journal as your dream hub—a space for you to capture all your wild ideas, determine your direction, and hatch a plan for each step. I think it will help you gain the clarity, confidence, and momentum you need to turn your ambitions into realities.

I've found that if I don't write down my thoughts and dreams, they can crowd up my headspace until I feel like my head will blow up. It's hard to make sense of it all and know what to act on. Or, if I don't write them down, they're like bad dogs running into the distance. You can whistle for them, but they're not coming back. When I heard that research shows people who write down their goals are 42 percent more likely to reach them,[1] I couldn't help but think of my dashboard Post-its and all the emails I send to myself daily. Those kinds of things keep me focused and energized and help me clarify my ideas. Whether you're charting out your next steps in this journal or scribbling reminders on your bathroom mirror, writing things down is going to help you too.

A lot of what you'll find here are the same kinds of prompts and exercises I use with groups in my Dream Big workshops. Thousands of people just like you have wrestled with these very things and have made great progress. I know you will too. And you'll even have the advantage of having a tool that will keep you on track—weekly wake-ups. If you're like me, you really have to fight off distractions to make progress. You have to go into beast mode and protect some time and energy each week for clearing the path toward your meaningful goals. These

1. Peter Economy, "This Is the Way You Need to Write Down Your Goals for Faster Success," Inc.com, February 28, 2018.

regular check-ins will help you carve new grooves in your brain and keep you awake to yourself and your bright future.

So grab your favorite pen and get ready to write. You'll be making lists, writing letters to yourself, answering some hard questions, and jotting down steps you can take to move toward your dream. The words you write here, in a way, are you. This is the good and hard work of understanding who you are and how God made you so you can unearth the ambitions that may have been sitting dormant in your heart. We're going to move them from staying inside of you to impacting the world around you.

Are you ready?

GOD IS OVER THE MOON ABOUT YOU

Right out of the gate, we've got to talk about this. How does God feel about you? Deep down, maybe you're not so sure.

Well, I am. I've asked Him. He's over the moon about you. He's not grimacing at your past failures; He's smiling at the bright future you have with Him.

You are loved and accepted. One hundred percent. No qualifications. No prerequisites. You can't be good enough, smart enough, or nice enough to be loved by God. He decided He would love you before you decided you were interested in loving Him back. Even if God is no big deal for you, your life is a big deal to Him. You are some of His most creative work ever.

Pursuing your ambitions needs to start from a position of acceptance, not compliance. Compliance only lasts until you decide you're not going to comply anymore. You won't be able to get to the best parts of your life and faith without accessing the best parts of acceptance.

Picture some of the moments in your life when you've felt absolutely loved and accepted. Write about them in detail here.

. . . .

. . . .

. . . .

. . . .

. . . .

You're probably doing a couple of things right and are a hot mess in other areas of your life. Me too. Accept it, but don't resign yourself to perpetually screwing up. You are in as much need of tremendous love and grace and kindness from God as we all are.

No matter what you do, God is love, and He loves and accepts you completely. So embrace His unreasonable amount of grace and acceptance. And then get ready to throw all you've got into your ambitions.

Acknowledge this reality in some way below. Personalize it. Repeat it. Respond to it and say how it impacts you.

. . . .

. . . .

. . . .

. . . .

. . . .

. . . .

. . . .

. . . .

TRAINING FOR ETERNITY

As you pursue your ambitions, you can rest in knowing that heaven is simply nuts about you and can't wait for you to get there. That said, you've got some time right here, so let's figure out how to make good use of it.

Early on in *Dream Big*, I said that our lives are on-the-job training for eternity. We're all practicing for heaven.

What does that mean to you?

. . . .

. . . .

. . . .

. . . .

. . . .

. . . .

If we want to lead lives full of meaning, we're going to have to trade what is easily available for what is actually worthwhile. I used to spend my time doing things that worked. Now I'm trying to do things that last.

What in your life right now would you say is lasting and worthwhile?

. . . .

. . . .

. . . .

. . . .

. . . .

. . . .

And here's one last biggie: What would you say is your life's purpose? This is a huge part of dreaming big, so really give this some thought.

....

....

....

....

....

....

....

....

....

....

"If you read history you will find that the Christians who did most for the present world were precisely those who thought most of the next."

—C. S. Lewis

--▷

ALL YOUR DAYS
BUILD A LEGACY

The farther along you go on this adventure called life, the more valuable experiences and insights you bring to your future. They're shaping what you value and what choices you want to make.

What valuable experiences and insights are you
bringing into your future?

....

....

....

....

....

....

....

....

....

....

....

You're evolving into a new version of you every
single day. All those days together will eventually tell
your life story. Your legacy will be the amount of love
and hope and engagement you release into the world,
your self-awareness and your other-awareness, and
your willingness to adapt and adopt new approaches
as you evolve.

If you could determine today what your life's legacy will be, how would you describe it?

. . . .

. . . .

. . . .

. . . .

. . . .

. . . .

In the coming weeks, we're going to dive deeper into who you are and what you want, but for now, sit with this:

- God derives tremendous joy when He sees you pursuing your unique desires with the skill set He put in your individual tool box.
- He's inviting you into a life that is more expansive and expressive, more loving and selfless.
- He wants you to reflect His character in what you want and have these desires dwarf anything else that gets in the way.

Do you have any thoughts or reactions to this?

....

....

....

....

....

....

....

....

....

....

....

....

....

....

....

....

....

....

---▷

AMBITION'S TWO HANDLES

If ambitions had two handles, they would be love and hope. There have never been two forces in the world more powerful than these. It's no surprise that early followers of Jesus changed their world through "labor prompted by love" and "endurance inspired by hope" (1 Thessalonians 1:3).

For years I've been working in high-conflict countries in the hopes of easing some of the pain and bringing a little hope and a few more opportunities to the children. Why? It has been one of my ambitions to help young kids, and in particular, young girls, to get the shot at life they deserve, not just get shot at. When you're exposed to something that connects with your passion, you make it an ambition to find a way to effect some change.

Think back over your life. When has love moved you to action? When has hope affected how you lived?

....

....

....

....

....

....

....

....

....

....

....

....

....

Describe the love and hope you have in your heart right now.

. . . .

. . . .

. . . .

. . . .

. . . .

. . . .

. . . .

. . . .

As you continue on your Dream Big journey, keep grabbing ahold of that love and hope and never let go.

"Where there is no hope there can be no endeavor."
—Samuel Johnson

"Love is the energy of life."
—Robert Browning

WEEK 5

INVITING MIRACLES

If you're a Bible reader, what stands out to you when you think about the miracles in the Bible?

. . . .

. . . .

. . . .

. . . .

. . . .

Write down a few things that have happened in your life that feel like God's miracles to you.

....

....

....

....

....

....

....

....

....

....

....

....

There are thirty-seven recorded miracles in the New Testament. I enter each day assuming there's a thirty-eighth miracle waiting for me if I'll fully engage life and the people around me with love, honesty, and an unreasonable, almost annoying heap of expectation.

What would happen in your life if you started doing the same? What would life look like if you peered around every corner, dug in every couch cushion, and looked under the bed to see how God has already been doing miracles for you?

....

....

....

....

....

....

....

....

Pursuing your ambitions will take a big dollop of trust. But guess what? God's got you. So take the risk. It's worth it.

"If God is your partner, make your plans BIG!"
—D. L. Moody

WEEK 6

FAITH IS WHAT YOU DO

One of the writers in the Bible named Paul nailed it when he said, "The only thing that counts is faith expressing itself through love." I agree. It's easy to mistake faith with all the doctrine you believe to be true. Faith, however, is what you do about what you believe.

What do you do about what you believe? How you choose to live out your days will eventually become how you're known and remembered.

If you looked at everything on an average Tuesday, what would it say about your faith?

. . . .

. . . .

. . . .

. . . .

. . . .

. . . .

. . . .

. . . .

. . . .

. . . .

. . . .

. . . .

. . . .

. . . .

. . . .

. . . .

. . . .

If you could change anything about what you wrote above, what would it be? What might happen in your life, and in other people's lives, if you had a more courageous faith?

....

....

....

....

....

....

....

....

....

....

....

> "When it comes to faith, what a living, creative, active, powerful thing it is."
> **—Martin Luther**

WHO ARE YOU?

There are a number of ways you could answer the question *Who are you?*

How would you answer it today?

....

....

....

....

Now, let's go a little deeper. Most of the things that drive us—big and small—usually have a place of origin far below the surface. You may not even know about these places or have taken the time to explore them.

An unexpectant life is one that is merely on repeat. A life lived in constant anticipation, on the other hand, is one willing to do a load of self-examination. If we can learn what the core motivations behind our actions are, we can figure out where they came from and take the actions necessary to make progress.

Are there some recurring themes in your behavior and choices? For instance, do you tend to act out of fear or a sense there will never be enough? Do you think *you* will never be enough? Do you live life out of a fake bravado or think you have to always please others?

Take some time to explore *why* you do what you do. It's okay if this takes more than a few minutes, especially if you're asking yourself these questions for the first time. Take as much time as you need to express what is real, honest, and true about you.

....
....
....
....
....
....
....
....
....
....
....
....
....

As you do this, don't be too hard on yourself. Jesus surrounded Himself with disciples who couldn't get the nets on the right side of the boat most of the time, and He was kind and never mean to them. When you're real and authentic with Him, He won't beat you up when you mess up because He's embarrassed by you; He'll embrace you because He loves you.

---◿

WHAT DID HE GIVE YOU?

Knowing your talents is a great starting point for thinking about your dream. Write down ten things about yourself that feel like your innate talents. Maybe you're naturally friendly or optimistic. Maybe you are great at geometry or have a heart for homeless people. Things like this may not seem like "talents" as our culture defines them. They're so innate to who you are that they just feel like second nature. But they are your talents. After you make your list, give yourself a high five. Oh, and if you're having trouble coming up with ten things, just ask a few people in your life what they think your talents are to give you some hints. My bet is that you'll have a list a lot longer than ten things.

. . . .

. . . .

. . . .

. . . .

. . . .

. . . .

. . . .

. . . .

. . . .

. . . .

. . . .

. . . .

. . . .

. . . .

. . . .

Some people think their talents are the only things making up their identity. They lean heavily on them for success or approval.

Do you think you've given your talents and gifts too much weight in your sense of self-worth? Explain.

....
....
....
....
....
....

Where do you get your sense of identity and self-worth? If you aspire to get it another way, what would it be?

....
....
....
....
....
....

How could overreliance on your talents give you a "false positive" that you're moving in the direction of your dream?

....

....

....

....

....

....

....

....

....

....

....

> "We are God's handiwork, created in Christ Jesus to do good works, which God prepared in advance for us to do."
> **—Ephesians 2:10**

WEEK 9

--▷

WHERE ARE YOU?

This question is one of the first interactions we see in the Bible between God and the people like us that He made. When it got weird, Adam and Eve forgot who they were and hid. When God asked *Where are you?*, He wasn't looking for a literal answer, of course. God knows everything, even if we don't understand or won't acknowledge it. He wasn't talking about longitude and latitude; He was addressing their state of mind. He wanted to know whether they knew where they were.

How would you answer this question today? Think biography, not geography. For example, are you confused about which major to choose? Do you feel stuck in your career choice but don't know how to change it? Are you up to your eyeballs in debt? Are you happy in your marriage or other important relationships? Obviously, there are a million and one questions we could ask. But I bet you already have a sense of where you are right now in your life. Most of us know the real answers to these probing questions, but we're afraid to actually say them.

Take some time to describe exactly where you are right now. Be brutally honest. It's okay if you're not completely jazzed by your answer. Just about everyone wants something to change in their life, including me.

. . . .

. . . .

. . . .

. . . .

. . . .

. . . .

....
....
....
....
....
....
....
....
....
....
....

Think of a close friend who you can get honest with, then complete this statement: "I'm meeting _____ at Starbucks to tell them exactly where I am right now." Then send the text or make the call to set up the time.

We can't get on the path toward our ambitions without figuring out where we are. What has felt like your resting place is now a starting line. If you have the honesty and guts for it, what you've been stuck in is what you'll be freed from.

--▷

YOUR HISTORY IS YOUR SHERPA

Soon, we'll dive into what you want for your life and get a starter list of ambitions going. But first, think on this: For years you've already been quietly curating your life without knowing it. You know what works and what doesn't. What lights you up and bums you out. What lasts and what disappears.

We need to figure out what you've come up with so far so we can figure out what to do next.

Think back over your life experiences and choices, and what they've taught you about yourself. What comes to mind? What works for you, what lights you up, what lasts?

....

....

....

....

....

....

....

....

....

....

....

....

....

....

Trust what you've learned already; let it be your Sherpa.

WHAT DO YOU WANT?

So much of dreaming big is about finding the right answers to this very question: What do you want? In this part of the journal, we're going to make a first attempt at creating a list of what you want. Do you want a bigger house? Do you want to make working the soup line a Christmas tradition? Do you want to hike the Pacific Crest Trail or finally get to Paris? Do you want to lose weight or reconcile with your dad? It can be all this and more.

Your list will be totally unique to you, and it will probably get you pretty excited. That's the point! Don't worry about "editing" the list to make it look more noble or holy. Just be honest. Think about every single thing you're dreaming about right now and get it on a list. You can write out your first ideas on the lines below, but I recommend getting even more space. Get a notebook with at least fifty blank pages. It's okay if you fill one of them or all of them. Just make sure to capture everything. Later on we'll work toward curating the list and arranging your dreams so they make a constellation of possibilities you can actually work toward.

For now, just write it all down. Have fun!

. . . .

. . . .

. . . .

. . . .

. . . .

. . . .

. . . .

....
....
....
....
....
....
....
....
....
....
....
....
....
....
....

"Trust me, heaven will be doing cartwheels if you will finally get real about what you really want."

—Bob

WHY DO YOU WANT WHAT YOU WANT?

The best engine to drive our ambitions is a strong sense of purpose. There's nothing really important about the vacation or the new pair of kicks or the convertible. You'll want and enjoy those only for a while; they're the short game. Don't confuse them with your ambitions. The long game is where your best ambitions reside.

At times, though, we find ourselves feeling disconnected from a strong sense of purpose. The meaning we're looking for can get lost behind a hedge of distractions, hurts, and disappointments.

What have these been for you?

. . . .

. . . .

. . . .

. . . .

. . . .

. . . .

When we're out of touch with what's meaningful, we pursue inputs that ultimately distract us from our lack of direction. At some point, though, even the distractions aren't enough. Or someone else screws it up for us, and we end up wounded and lost again.

The fix isn't easy, but it's this simple: We need to replace what we've settled for with what we've been longing for. We need to find ambitions worthy of our time and the effort it will take to pursue them.

What have you settled for, and what have you been longing for?

. . . .

. . . .

. . . .

. . . .

. . . .

. . . .

Think of your most beautiful, lasting ambitions. Why do you want them?

. . . .

. . . .

. . . .

. . . .

. . . .

. . . .

. . . .

. . . .

. . . .

How are your ambitions connected to your life's purpose and training for eternity?

Fill in the circles to get a visual: Write your life purpose and what has eternal value in the outer circles. Write your ambition in the middle circle. Then describe how they are all connected in more detail on the next page.

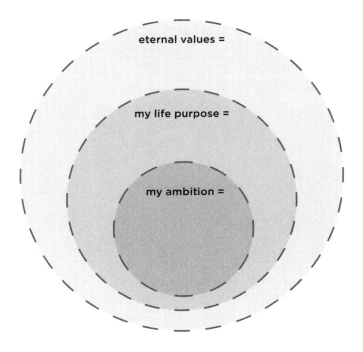

eternal values =

my life purpose =

my ambition =

. . . .

. . . .

. . . .

. . . .

. . . .

. . . .

. . . .

. . . .

. . . .

. . . .

. . . .

. . . .

. . . .

. . . .

. . . .

. . . .

You're establishing some possible targets for yourself now. Do you want them badly enough to do what it takes to reach them?

WHO DO YOU WANT TO BECOME?

We've been talking about living a life steeped in purpose, and this week we're going to look at another approach to finding that life. This one is all about identifying who you want to be and letting that inform what you do. You decide you'll no longer settle for what you're simply able to do; instead, you'll figure out what you were made to do, then do lots of that.

It's no simple task to understand what God made you for. Even once you know how God wired you, your ambitions will evolve and build over time. Remember why I've had lots of careers and done many different things? Because I'm constantly changing. You are as well. You have to stay current with yourself. Don't be who you were; be who you're becoming.

When you think about who you want to become, what comes to mind?

. . . .

. . . .

. . . .

. . . .

. . . .

. . . .

. . . .

I'm sure God's not asking you to mimic someone else, but other people can inspire you to discover your own beautiful ambition and chase after new things.

Who inspires you?

....

....

....

....

....

....

What if "future you" could write a letter to "current you" about all you've accomplished and experienced on this journey? What would that future you say to help and encourage the current you? Take fifteen to twenty minutes to write that letter. Stuff it in an envelope, address it to yourself, and put a date on it that's a few months into the future. Six months is a pretty good stretch. That's the day you're going to open and read the letter.

"What you are is God's gift to you, what you become is your gift to God."
—Hans Urs von Balthasar

51

--▷

GIVE JESUS THE WHOLE ROOM

You're a lot farther along than when you first began this Dream Big journey. You've got a big list of ambitions and have discovered some God-given dreams in your heart. Now what?

You've got to activate your faith in order to drive your life.

Jesus wants you to align your faith with your

talents and chase after your ambitions. He wants you to stare down your fears knowing He's got your back and can handle anything that comes your way. But none of that can happen if you don't invite Him into every part of your life.

Jesus is knocking on the door of your life not to just have you take a safe look at Him through a peephole or give Him a little bit of closet space. He wants the whole room and everything in it— including you. The problem is, your life may already be fully occupied.

To begin with, have you "answered the door"? What is your response to Jesus' knocking? Have you given Him the whole room, or are you trying to cram Him in a corner?

. . . .

. . . .

. . . .

. . . .

. . . .

. . . .

What do you need to get rid of in your life to make
space for Jesus?

....

....

....

....

....

....

....

How would your faith transform if you gave Him the
space He wants to be the center of your life?

....

....

....

....

....

....

....

....

Imagine taking everything you pursue—good grades, a better job, a house in a different neighborhood, a boyfriend, whatever—and laying them out on the table.

How are these things flowing into your life of faith?

....
....
....
....
....
....
....
....
....
....
....
....

Now imagine taking those things one by one and deciding whether you should add them back to your faith and your life.

Should you move something from the table to the
"garbage bin"? What would you add back?

---▷

BELIEVE IN HIS LOVE

One of the hardest things to believe about God is that He loves you completely and unconditionally. Are you having any trouble with that at this point in your Dream Big journey?

Is there anything lurking in your heart that says you have to change, be better, or do something different to earn God's love?

....
....
....
....
....
....

How would a complete and enduring belief in God's
love change your life and fuel your dream right now?

....
....
....
....
....
....

You're going to have to become a ninja at spotting anything in your way that is counter to God's love and is selling you a bill of goods that makes you question whether you're absolutely loved and accepted by Him.

Write out a few examples of this, then cross them out.

. . . .

. . . .

. . . .

. . . .

Let's practice a little situational awareness. Answer these questions:

- Am I feeling safe, supported, known?

  _____

- Am I expressing myself authentically, or have my interactions felt artificial and contrived?

  _____

- Am I saying what I really think, or am I channeling someone else's explanation about life that I don't fully believe?

. . . .

. . . .

. . . .

. . . .

Even if this feels a little foreign, carve that new groove in your brain and ask yourself these questions more often. People who achieve their ambitions are constantly doing this. It becomes so natural that after a while they're unaware they're doing it anymore. It just becomes part of how they roll.

If you're struggling, come back to what you know is true. God's love really is unconditional. He's saying, "I love you completely, no matter what. Be strong and courageous. Be fully alive." What else is God telling you?

....

....

....

....

....

....

....

....

....

....

---▷

IT'S TIME TO WAKE UP

If you want to make progress toward your ambitions, you can't walk around half awake. It's possible that you've slipped into some numbing routines that are putting you to sleep and keeping you stuck. Let's take a look.

Think about your daily routine. Is it a good one—one worth repeating? Does it have too strong a grip on your life? Is it keeping you from advancing on to your newer, more beautiful ambitions?

....
....
....
....
....
....
....
....
....

Sometimes we go through our days doing all the things we've committed to or that were expected of us without really "checking in" with ourselves. How often do you ask yourself questions like these?

- How am I feeling?
- Does God feel near?
- Am I living out my top priorities and most beautiful ambitions through my choices and actions?

If you're sleepwalking through your life, you may need to do something startling to shake yourself awake. I'm not suggesting you blow up your whole life. But who knows, maybe you do need to switch your job or major, or make a change in a relationship. Maybe you need to break a routine or enlist some kind of help.

What possibilities come to mind?

. . . .

. . . .

. . . .

. . . .

For me, meeting new people stokes new perspectives and curiosity. Understanding how others have lived their lives will awaken something inside of you too. I also recommend getting more tuned in to your faith, family, and friends. A lot can happen when you pay more attention to what you're engaged in.

Don't underestimate the power of shaking things up.

What will you do this week to become more fully alive?

....
....
....
....
....
....
....
....
....
....
....
....
....
....
....
....
....

---◁▷

AVAILABILITY AND ENGAGEMENT

The adventure on your way toward your ambitions is going to require a new level of interest in the people around you. Why? Because availability is the most reliable predictor of engagement, and engagement is the most reliable predictor of success. Availability keeps you open to the world around you so you don't fall back asleep, and it can be a huge multiplier in your life—more people, invitations, ideas.

Here's something else to remember: ambitions don't flow from the quantity of our ideas or our uninterrupted drive; they gush out from our kindness and willingness to take a genuine interest in others.

What are your reactions to this statement? Describe any examples of this you've experienced or seen in others' lives.

. . . .

. . . .

. . . .

. . . .

. . . .

. . . .

. . . .

. . . .

. . . .

. . . .

. . . .

A lot of people are constantly looking at others and silently asking the question *What can this person do for me?* What about you and your daily life? Are you scanning the room to size up what you can get from the people around you?

How would your life change if you flipped the script and instead asked, *What can I give to everyone here?*

....

....

....

....

....

....

....

....

....

....

....

....

....

Does it seem strange or possibly even counter-productive to your dream to think how you can find opportunities for others? Are you afraid that if you give too much, there won't be anything left over for yourself?

. . . .

. . . .

. . . .

. . . .

. . . .

. . . .

. . . .

Have you ever been in a position to open a path of possibility for someone else? How did it feel to play the role of giver instead of receiver?

. . . .

. . . .

. . . .

. . . .

. . . .

List three people in your life to whom you could become more available. What will you do today and this week to make yourself more available in their lives?

....

....

....

....

....

....

....

....

....

....

....

"The people you spend time with will play the largest part in the ambitions you achieve, not the minutes you saved each day by avoiding them."
—Bob

WEEK 18

REACH OUT A WEAKER, MORE AUTHENTIC HAND

People are essential on the journey to your ambitions. Without others to help, encourage, and support you, it'll be difficult (and probably impossible) to achieve your dream. And the more authentic you are with yourself and with others, the better.

This can be hard for some of us to accept. Are you the kind of person who thinks they need to go it alone?

Does help from someone else feel uncomfortable to accept? If so, why?

. . . .

. . . .

. . . .

. . . .

. . . .

. . . .

. . . .

Take a moment and list five people in your life who are your friends.

. . . .

. . . .

. . . .

. . . .

. . . .

. . . .

. . . .

. . . .

. . . .

As you look at each name, can you remember the last time you asked each of them a probing question that got past the surface? Star each name for whom the answer is yes.

Now, think about yourself with each of these people. Can you remember the last time you shared something that felt vulnerable and real? You might recall how I described finally reaching out my shaky left hand in a prayer circle after repeatedly concealing it. When have you reached out a weaker, more authentic hand?

Describe it here.

. . . .

. . . .

. . . .

. . . .

. . . .

. . . .

. . . .

. . . .

. . . .

In general, would you say you're a person who is willing to go deep with others?

....
....
....
....
....
....
....
....
....
....
....
....
....
....
....

Make a big effort to be authentic and available in the coming week.

Try to have real conversations during the next week.
Then come back and write about what happened.

> "The trick to leading a noteworthy life
> is having noteworthy conversations and
> writing down what you learn. Do lots of
> that and opportunities will find you."
> **—Bob**

---▷

REST IS WISE

Anyone can fall into the trap of thinking that work equals progress. In some sense, I guess that's true if you're doing the right things. But you can get so laser-focused on what you want to accomplish that you end up grinding yourself into a fine powder with all your hustle.

Some days need to be about gathering strength instead of exerting it. Constant activity will not only leave you winded but also can get you sleepwalking again.

Do you have rhythms in your life that allow you to get adequate rest? Do you sleep enough? Do you work compulsively and realize too late that you're burned out?

. . . .

. . . .

. . . .

. . . .

. . . .

. . . .

. . . .

. . . .

. . . .

. . . .

. . . .

How can you pursue rest today and this week? How can you build rest into the rhythms of your life?

. . . .

. . . .

. . . .

. . . .

. . . .

. . . .

. . . .

. . . .

. . . .

. . . .

. . . .

. . . .

. . . .

. . . .

. . . .

. . . .

> "It's easy to confuse a lot of activity with a bunch of progress. Rest is wise. Don't think that taking care of yourself means you're slacking."
>
> **—Bob**

---➢

COMPARISON IS A PUNK

I f you want to do something that honors God, you can't try to be someone else. You've got to be you.

Understand *your* ambitions. Own them. Take aim at them. Confusing someone else's dreams for your own, or thinking your dreams should be more like theirs, will cost you the prize. Every. Single. Time.

Have you found yourself aiming for somebody else's target?

....

....

....

....

....

....

....

....

It's easy to fall into the trap of thinking you have to do things the way everyone else did. It's also tempting to think someone else had an easier path with smaller obstacles than the ones you're facing. Who knows, maybe they did. Chasing after your dreams requires clearheadedness and wide eyes that are trained to follow the specific path in front of you, not the path in front of them.

Are you the kind of person who thinks everyone else has it better than you or has it more together than you?

List some ways that you struggle to "keep your eyes on your own paper" in your own life.

. . . .

. . . .

. . . .

. . . .

. . . .

. . . .

. . . .

God made you uniquely gifted. So go run your own race.

How can you picture yourself doing this?

. . . .

. . . .

. . . .

. . . .

. . . .

. . . .

. . . .

Look into the mirror a couple of times a day at that beautiful, God-given mug of yours and tell yourself over and over until you believe it that God never wondered if you had everything you needed to be fully you. We need to get you on board with the idea that you are a wonderfully creative, totally fallible, gifted, easily distractible, once-ever-in-history you.

"Listen closely. Your best is enough."
—Bob

WEEK 21

---◔▷

GET HONEST AND SPECIFIC

Look back at the big list of ambitions you started a while ago (pages 40–41). Does your list feel like you, or are there some impostors hanging out in there? Before you move forward in this journal, make sure your list is honest and genuine. Your list should feel like an autobiography of who you are and what you really want. Revisit your list and revise as needed. Is there anything you need to add or take off? Remember, there are not right or wrong moves here. The only thing that matters is that your list is honest and truly reflects you.

Write down any thoughts and reactions here.

....
....
....
....
....
....
....

This is a hard question, but I have to ask. Are you looking to get a pat on your back for some items on your list? Do you want your teacher or pastor to see it so you can feel affirmed? Do you want your spouse or best friend to think you've made the right choices? Be honest. If something on your list feels like someone else's fulfilled expectation of you—but not necessarily a genuine dream of your own—take some time to think on it.

Why did you add it? Should you just let go of it? The last thing we want is you chasing a dream you think you're supposed to have but don't actually have.

. . . .

. . . .

. . . .

. . . .

. . . .

. . . .

Are there some items on your list that are too vague? If they're not specific enough, you'll never know if you actually achieved them. Go through your list and drill down to get really concrete about your ambitions.

Which ones need to be more specific, and how?

. . . .

. . . .

. . . .

. . . .

. . . .

SIZE UP YOUR AMBITIONS

I f you're going to get some movement on your dreams, you'll have to create some priorities. You can't chase them all at the same time—nor should you. Take the list you have (pages 40–41) and create three different categories: small, medium, and large. Place everything on your list in one of these categories. Don't worry about doing this exactly right. The exercise is more about clarifying what you can pursue quickly or what might take some time. (See chart on page 94.)

For each of your "large" dreams, answer these three questions:

- Is it meaningful? (Does this dream reflect my most beautiful values and hopes?)
- Will it last? (Will this dream stand the test of time? Will it last my lifetime or even past my lifetime?)
- Will it help others? (Is this dream just another feather in my cap, or will it impact the people around me? Remember, scale doesn't matter— there just needs to be a blast radius of goodness to your dream.)

Which of your "large" ambitions gets a yes to all three questions?

. . . .

. . . .

. . . .

. . . .

. . . .

. . . .

Now, looking at the "small" dreams, draw a line if one of those dreams seems connected or could lead to a "medium" or "large" dream.

Write any thoughts about those possible connections here.

. . . .

. . . .

. . . .

. . . .

. . . .

. . . .

. . . .

. . . .

. . . .

. . . .

As you marshal your ambitions, don't rush the process. It could take an hour or a month. Some people get clarity on their ambitions waiting in the drive-through line; others go on a weekend retreat. Do whatever works for you.

Find ambitions that will positively impact the lives of others and get you fired up to pursue a few more ambitions for yourself. If you're going to spend your time, talent, and treasure to get some of those dreams off the ground, isn't it worth the investment of time and conviction to find the right ones?

SMALL	MEDIUM	LARGE

KNOW YOUR OBSTACLES

The dreams you wrote down and vetted made it on your list because you haven't accomplished them yet. Why? Are you the kind of person who needs a fully reliable master plan before you take the first step? Are you stopped before you begin because of fear of what others might think? Maybe you have a family or a full-time job and can't carve out the time to make some moves toward your dreams.

We're not creating solutions for these obstacles just yet. Identifying them, though, is an important step. (We'll get to the solution part later.)

Take a moment to write out what has kept you from pursuing your dreams.

....
....
....
....
....
....
....
....
....
....
....

I've spent years effecting change in war-torn areas of the world. There is plenty of conflict and uncertainty in those places, but there is also boatloads of hope. Some people actively look for hope even in the midst of chaos or difficulty. Be one of these people. The reason is simple. We all find what we spend the most time looking for.

Don't get wrapped around the axle despairing that your ambitions haven't been achieved yet. Delight in the fact that you have a couple of things worth doing that you haven't gotten to yet. Cultivate a spirit of hope and live in constant anticipation of what might become possible in your life if you start looking at things differently.

Complete a few sentences that begin with something like, "I have hope that . . ." or "I know I can . . ."

....

....

....

....

....

....

....

....

....

CHASE ONE DREAM

When you look at your list of dreams, you need to find the one that lights you up the most. Working toward your dreams comes with some opportunity costs. Choosing one dream to chase means you might have to wait on another. You have to be incredibly picky about how you spend your time, energy, and resources.

When you look at your list, is anything sticking out that may not be worth it? Is there one large dream that leads the pack and gets you most excited?

. . . .

. . . .

. . . .

. . . .

. . . .

Once you've got one ambition in sight, a real practical way to get some quick momentum is research. I know it sounds boring, but it won't be. You'll be lapping up Google searches, I promise.

What questions do you need answers to?

. . . .

. . . .

. . . .

. . . .

. . . .

Think about the body of knowledge you'll need to accomplish your dream.

What steps can you take to start learning what you'll need to know when your dream is fully realized?

....

....

....

....

....

You'll probably have your own unique path between where you are and where you want to be.

What are a few paths you can imagine?

....

....

....

....

....

This week, start doing your homework. Think about how you can tune your life to your ambition and begin inserting yourself where it can be fulfilled. Here are some ideas to get you started—mark any you'll do:

- ☐ Get to know some of the names in your desired space.
- ☐ Follow them on social media and join the conversation.
- ☐ Set a Google alert so you receive an email every time the person comes up in the news. It's like non-creepy stalking.
- ☐ Find and get familiar with a few websites related to your ambition.

What else will you add to the list?

. . . .

. . . .

. . . .

. . . .

> "Do what you can, with what you have, where you are."
> **—Teddy Roosevelt**

EXPLORE OPPORTUNITIES

It's time to start finding and following the breadcrumb trails to your one big dream.

Exploring opportunities takes focused intentionality. *Is this person I met a part of the journey? That article looks like it might have some ideas for me. I sense I need to attend that new church for a few Sundays.* These are the types of breadcrumb trails people follow when they're on the scent of their big dreams.

Name three people you know right now who could help you make some progress on your dream. Are you willing to approach them and ask for help? If so, how and when will you do that?

....

....

....

....

....

Name three people you want to know who can help you toward your dream. Is there a way you can get to them? Can you find their phone numbers and give them a call? What about their email addresses? How far are you willing to go to get an audience with someone who could be key for you to accomplish your dream?

....

....

....

....

....

What conferences could you attend? Picture yourself (politely) muscling your way to the front of the line and introducing yourself to people.

. . . .

. . . .

. . . .

. . . .

List anything else you can think of that you could do to get closer to your dream.

. . . .

. . . .

. . . .

. . . .

Now, pick the one thing you'll do next to get some forward movement. It's tempting to write down a sequence of events like lining up dominoes. But I find that it's really empowering to have one thing that you can do to move your dream forward. (Of course, once that's done you can write down the next thing. Eventually you'll have a daisy chain of completed steps!)

Write down that one thing.

. . . .

. . . .

. . . .

. . . .

. . . .

. . . .

. . . .

. . . .

. . . .

. . . .

. . . .

"People committed to their ambitions don't wait for doors to open. They knock, then they ring the doorbell, then they camp out. They remain attentive while assuming they are invited to their ambitions rather than waiting endlessly for permission."

—Bob

CALL OUT CAPTORS AND LIMITING BELIEFS

You can't move forward with your new ambitions without sloughing off some of your old hang-ups, and you can't simply walk away from these hang-ups without understanding them first. What's underneath the surface and holding you back? See what you can find there, and then break your relationship with it. You can turn whatever has been holding you hostage into a path toward freedom.

In *Dream Big* I told a story about a bank robbery that led to something we now call Stockholm syndrome.

Why do you think we cling to our captors, the things holding us hostage in our lives?

. . . .

. . . .

. . . .

. . . .

. . . .

. . . .

. . . .

. . . .

As you scan the current dynamics in your life—both internal and external—do you have anything you would say is holding you hostage? If so, how strong is its hold in your life?

Take a few minutes to write down some thoughts if you feel you need to name your captors and call them out for the roles they play in keeping you hostage.

....

....

....

....

....

Were you raised with any limiting beliefs from your parents? Were you continuously told year after year by a teacher, pastor, coach, or friend what it takes to be accepted? Maybe you have come to believe certain narratives in your life as "universal truths" about who you are.

If so, what are those, and where did they come from?

....

....

....

....

....

Now, having identified any limiting beliefs, how might they be standing in the way of some audacious dreams you have or want to have but are too hesitant to chase?

....

....

....

....

....

....

....

....

....

....

....

Listen up. You are not a hostage anymore.

So will you let limiting beliefs keep grabbing the microphone in your life, possibly until the day you die? Or will you silence those old voices telling you lies about yesterday so the truth of today becomes more audible?

---▷

GIVE POWER TO LAUNCHING BELIEFS

My grandparents had me convinced my entire young life that I was the most fun, engaging, amazing, creative, and winsome person ever to live. These became launching beliefs (the opposite of limiting beliefs) for me and were the birthplace of most of the joy I've found for the rest of my life.

--▷

What is your version of that? Which voices in your life have been most encouraging, and what did they say? What moments meant the most to you?

. . . .

. . . .

. . . .

. . . .

. . . .

. . . .

. . . .

. . . .

. . . .

. . . .

Are there any launching beliefs that you can be grateful for and focus on as you make moves toward your dreams? Think of at least three positive things people have consistently said about you during your life. Maybe you're a natural optimist or selfless or a hard worker. Maybe you have some natural skills and abilities that have consistently caught other people's attention.

Write about them here.

....

....

....

....

....

....

....

....

....

....

....

....

....

....

Next, create some reminders on sticky notes (or your phone lock screen or written on your bathroom mirror, or wherever you look often) to help you remember what is inherently good and true about you.

DO IT SCARED

Fear is a part of all our lives. Even the most fearless among us have to stare it down and decide to act anyway. On a scale of one to ten—with one being "very little" and ten being "all the time"—how much does fear have a hold of your life?

On the line below, mark the level of fear in your life.

1	2	3	4	5	6	7	8	9	10

VERY LITTLE   ALL THE TIME

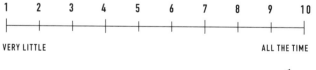

Our limiting beliefs usually take the shape of fear. This can manifest as procrastination, rationalizing, busyness, and a host of other subconscious tactics we employ to keep from chasing our ambitions. Fear boxes us in and will always try to talk us into settling for lesser things. If we let fear push us around, it won't be long before we're all fences and no horses.

We'll never start living our own authentic lives.

Have you ever heard the phrase "do it scared"? I heard once that courage isn't the absence of fear but the willingness to act in the face of fear. Think back to times in your life when you did something even though you were scared.

What were your thoughts? What were your actions? What were the results?

. . . .

. . . .

. . . .

. . . .

. . . .

. . . .

When you think about the role of fear in your life, what are you willing to do to overcome this emotion when it comes to your big dreams?

....

....

....

....

....

....

....

....

"Do one thing every day that scares you."
—Eleanor Roosevelt

---✈

YOU HAVE A TON OF AGENCY

Who you are right now is an accumulation of all you've done and all that's happened to you. You may like who you see in the mirror, or maybe you have a few bones to pick. If you're like me, it's probably a little of both. You've made some choices, and they probably didn't all turn out the way you hoped. Don't worry; that's true for all of us. We're in a constant state of becoming the next version of us—and that's a good thing.

Remember that on this journey of discovering and launching your dream, you have a ton of agency over your circumstances. You can't change what happened yesterday or five minutes ago. But tomorrow is all yours, and it's up to you to decide what happens next.

Describe three examples of times in your life when you've taken initiative in a big way.

. . . .

. . . .

. . . .

. . . .

. . . .

What were the results, both short-term and long-term?

. . . .

. . . .

. . . .

. . . .

. . . .

I've made a lot of pivots in my life. I've painted houses, pumped gas, and parked cars. I've created safe houses and schools and an airline. I'm a lawyer, a speaker, an author, a diplomat, and many more things.

I never installed a circuit breaker to shut down my ambitions when they seemed improbable or when the results of my efforts looked uncertain. Instead, I gave myself license to pursue all the available opportunities I could find. You can too. You just need to keep your eyes open to opportunities and put yourself into the stream of possibility.

List ways you have agency related to chasing your ambitions right now.

. . . .

. . . .

. . . .

. . . .

. . . .

. . . .

. . . .

What will you do next?

....

....

....

....

....

....

....

....

CLEAR THE PATH

When I've spoken to people about their dreams, one of the most common reasons people tell me their dreams can't happen is all the commitments they currently have and can't let go of. I get it. I've made commitments that seemed good at the time but ended up shackling me to a particular spot.

What commitments have you made that take up time, space, and energy on a daily or weekly basis?

. . . .

. . . .

. . . .

. . . .

. . . .

. . . .

What would happen if you picked one thing— really, just one—and decided to stop doing it? Maybe it's something as big as a letter of resignation or something as simple as paying for school lunch one day a week instead of packing it. My hunch is you can let go of more than you believe you can.

Pick one thing and just see what happens. Write about it here.

. . . .

. . . .

. . . .

. . . .

Imagine how much extra time, space, and energy you would have for your dreams if you decided you were in charge of your commitments. I'm not suggesting you ditch everyone and become unreliable. It's important to keep your word. But you also have permission to change and shift, to adapt and be nimble.

Describe a day in the near future when you've dropped some of the burdens you're currently carrying and replaced them with activities that move you closer to a fulfilled dream.

. . . .

. . . .

. . . .

. . . .

. . . .

. . . .

. . . .

. . . .

. . . .

---◁▷

QUITTING TIME

Thursday is coming. It happens every week, so you know you can rely on it. Name one thing you're going to quit this Thursday. It could be a chore or a job or a daily routine. It could be a volunteer position or a habit or negative attitude. It could be anything, really, just something you decide isn't helping you anymore.

Go ahead—write down the thing you'll quit, then mark your calendar for this Thursday.

....

....

....

....

....

....

....

....

....

....

....

Saying no is not a pleasant experience for most people. But it's a critical skill if you're going to save space for your dreams. Often, we just need a little practice saying no. Go practice saying no one hundred times in the bathroom mirror. Get a few close friends together and have a "no" party where you practice with one another. Step out on your front porch and yell it at the top of your lungs.

What are a few common occurrences in your life where you just can't seem to say no?

....
....
....
....
....
....
....
....
....
....
....
....
....
....

Now, make a plan to decline the next time. The truth is, people respect it when you tell them no in the right way. It really is a liberating and powerful tool on your journey toward your dream.

LIVE ON THE EDGE
OF YIKES

When was the last time you left your comfort zone?

It's natural to seek comfort and familiarity in life. A life filled with uncertainty can feel too chaotic and stressful. Just the right amount of stress, however, can awaken our senses and bring out some of our best traits. This tension is almost always part of chasing a dream.

Are you afraid of living on the edge of yikes? Does it get you completely amped and ready to take on the world?

Describe your default reaction as you start to take some steps toward your dreams.

. . . .

. . . .

. . . .

. . . .

. . . .

. . . .

. . . .

. . . .

. . . .

. . . .

I've discovered that comfortable people don't need Jesus and don't chase their ambitions—desperate people do. If you're going to chase your ambitions, you'll have to be willing to get uncomfortable. Even desperate.

How is your life comfortable right now? What familiar and predictable parts might be holding you back?

....

....

....

....

....

....

....

Living on the edge of yikes can be scary and hard, and it's sometimes even painful. That's okay. Keep breathing. Stay after it. Move toward your edge where Jesus is waiting for you. God's not leading us to the safest path forward but to the one where we'll grow the most.

> "To venture causes anxiety, but not
> to venture is to lose one's self."
> **—Søren Kierkegaard**

YOU'RE HERE, YOU'RE ALIVE, YOU'RE ABLE

As you know, I started schools and created safe houses in war-torn countries. I didn't wait for an invitation to do those things. Guess what? You don't need an invitation to pursue your ambitions either. You're here, you're alive, and you're able. That's all the invitation you need.

Have you been waiting for more of an invitation?

Jesus never told anyone to play it safe. You were born to be brave. So act like it. Live into this truth. If you want some of your ambitions to take a leap forward, you need to get out of the safe-and-predictable zone and take a couple of risks.

What are some possible risks ahead on your Dream Big journey?

. . . .

. . . .

. . . .

. . . .

. . . .

. . . .

. . . .

. . . .

. . . .

. . . .

. . . .

. . . .

. . . .

How do you want to handle those risks? Try including some statements that start with something like, "I will be courageous and . . ."

. . . .

. . . .

. . . .

. . . .

. . . .

. . . .

. . . .

. . . .

. . . .

. . . .

Do something. Descend the cliff. Paddle through the waves. Don't sit on the sidelines; get in the game. There's no way your ambition can take flight without you taking action. Don't think about the mistakes you might make; think about the beauty you'll see. You're only about a minute away from seeing what's next.

---‐▷

YOUR NEXT ACTION STEPS

Okay, it's time to go Grand Canyon on your ambition. Let's get focused and make some concrete plans to move you toward your dream.

Here are a few ideas to get started:

- Post a list of your ambitions.
- Make a date with yourself (to reserve time for focusing on your ambitions).
- Make one phone call a day.

◁‐⋯

- Set incremental milestones.
- Put reminders everywhere.
- Get some administrative help.
- _____
- _____

Mark the ideas above that resonate with you. Do you have a few tricks and tactics you already use? Add them to the list above.

Now, write out in detail what specific things you want to do and decide in advance when and how you're going to do them.

. . . .

. . . .

. . . .

. . . .

. . . .

. . . .

. . . .

. . . .

. . . .

....

....

....

....

....

....

....

....

....

....

....

Next, put them on your calendar. Have a friend call you to check that you actually did it. Whatever it takes, decide now that you're going to act.

> "The most important thing in life is to stop saying 'I wish' and start saying 'I will.'"
> **—Charles Dickens**

PUSH BACK AGAINST RESISTANCE

You might be able to divide the world between people who procrastinate and those who don't. It's the late-night crammers versus the people who studied for weeks before the big test. Be honest with yourself—are you a procrastinator? _____ Do you think of a dozen reasons why not to get started?

Think back to times in your life when you didn't procrastinate. Why didn't you? What were the actions you took?

....

....

....

....

....

....

....

....

....

....

....

....

....

....

Decide now how you're going to respond to any impulse to procrastinate as you take your next steps toward your dream.

Describe how you're going to respond.

. . . .

. . . .

. . . .

. . . .

. . . .

. . . .

. . . .

Sometimes the resistance we feel toward action comes from inside us. Other times it comes from the people around us.

Can you name one or two people who you think will try to tamp down your dream?

. . . .

. . . .

. . . .

. . . .

. . . .

. . . .

145

How will you respond when they start to douse your attempts?

....

....

....

....

....

....

....

....

....

"Be strong and courageous."
—Deuteronomy 31:6

"Do not fear, for I am with you. . . .
I will strengthen you and help you."
—Isaiah 41:10

TAKING ACTION = ACCEPTING MISTAKES

Perfectionism can be a major roadblock to our dreams. We think, *If I can't do it exactly how I want, I won't do it at all*. Don't fall prey to this. Are you a perfectionist who does less because it won't be exactly right the first time? _____

Think back to some times when you totally flubbed up, or didn't quite reach the mark, and things still eventually turned out okay.

Write about those experiences.

....

....

....

....

....

....

....

....

....

....

....

....

....

....

Your actions from this point forward will not be perfect either. Often, not even close. But remind yourself that's okay. Whatever your ambition is, keep at it. Will it work? Who knows? Fail trying; don't fail watching.

Imagine a few imperfections and mistakes that could be part of your next step toward your ambitions. Go ahead and name them.

....

....

....

....

....

Now, imagine good things that could result from you trying, even if you mess up.

....

....

....

....

> "The important work of moving
> the world forward does not wait
> to be done by perfect men."
> **—George Eliot**

KICK YOUR FEARS
IN THE TEETH

When I hear from people struggling to realize their dreams, fear of failure comes up over and over. Earlier in this journal we talked about fear, but we're going to return to it this week because staring down fears is something we have to do continually on the Dream Big journey.

Which fears are driving you today?

....
....
....
....
....
....
....
....
....
....
....
....

Here's a hard truth you need to keep in mind about your fears: they will not go away by themselves. They're more likely to multiply like rabbits in the dark. Listen up. Fears don't really get fully conquered; they're just understood and given less power.

Be strong and courageous. Are you willing to slay the dragon to move toward your ambition? _____

Today, what would it mean for you to kick your fears in the teeth and get back to work?

....

....

....

....

....

....

....

....

....

....

....

"The Spirit God gave us does not make us timid,
but gives us power, love and self-discipline."
—2 Timothy 1:7

LEAN INTO FAILURE

When you fail epically, you're not alone.

Truthfully, most people are more concerned about others seeing them fail than they are about actually failing. So we all, to some degree, try to act like we're not failing at all—ever. We wonder, are we the only one having big and small failures pockmark our days?

Don't be tricked into thinking you're the only one having to trudge through difficulties.

In the diagram below, name people in each category who failed and later succeeded.

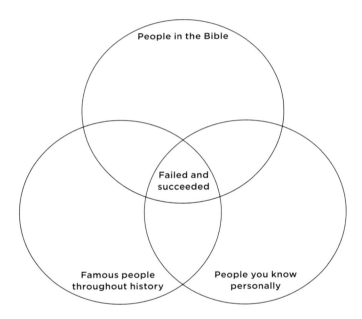

What do these examples tell you?

. . . .

. . . .

. . . .

. . . .

. . . .

. . . .

. . . .

. . . .

. . . .

. . . .

. . . .

We all need to get more comfortable with failure, because it's a reality for all of us. You could even consider failing on purpose just to get it out of your system. You have to accept that not every attempt toward your dream will be successful.

So many good people with great ideas never take their ideas out of the hangar, while other folks eventually see their ambitions become a reality. The one difference between them is a willingness to fail.

The next time you fail, how do you want to respond? Take a few minutes and write a paragraph or two.

....

....

....

....

....

....

....

....

....

....

....

....

....

....

....

....

---▷

SETBACKS REVEAL
AND EQUIP

I told a story about Sweet Maria after our Lodge burned down. I learned something powerful and precious about her in the wake of that loss. It made the catastrophe worth every singed beam and piece of timber.

Have you experienced some setbacks and simply tried to power through or get past the pain as quickly as possible? Take a moment and sit in the heap.

.--▷

What can you learn about yourself that only setbacks can help reveal?

. . . .

. . . .

. . . .

. . . .

. . . .

. . . .

. . . .

. . . .

. . . .

. . . .

. . . .

. . . .

Sometimes our setbacks make us more qualified, not less. Think about your life and some attempts that didn't go as planned. Maybe you faceplanted or lost some money or hurt someone you cared about. But with a little distance from the setback, you also gained some authority to help others avoid the same.

Can you recall a time in your life when a difficult experience equipped you to help someone else avoid the same mistake?

....

....

....

....

....

....

....

Can you recall a time when a past setback helped you avoid the same mistake?

....

....

....

....

....

....

....

Describe your relationship with failure at this point in your Dream Big journey. Do you still avoid it at all costs? If so, why? What do you fear about failing?

....

....

....

....

....

....

....

....

....

....

> "On the other side of an epic fail can be equally epic beauty and authenticity, which can only be born out of understanding our desperate need for love, grace, and help."
> **—Bob**

---▷

GET BUSY GETTING BETTER

The place where faith and failure meet can be tricky. You've probably heard people say "God opened the door" or "God closed the door." Maybe you're one of them. It's tempting to interpret our setbacks as heavenly signals we're headed in the wrong direction. I don't think this is true, because the dreams we have, I believe, are God-given gifts. How about you?

Do you tend to think any blip along the way is God speaking to you in code? If so, why?

. . . .

. . . .

. . . .

. . . .

. . . .

. . . .

. . . .

. . . .

. . . .

Failure can be as simple as this: what you tried just didn't work out the way you hoped. So don't bail out. Figure out what the problem is and change your approach. Don't conjure up divine intervention for the wrong strategy or for poor performance. Get busy getting better.

You're going to have setbacks and obstacles in all forms and sizes. Big, public, debilitating ones. Small, annoying, more pedestrian ones. What you need to do is figure out how to frame each one in the overall arc of the pursuit of your ambitions.

We'll practice. Name a setback or obstacle you've dealt with in the past. Then write out several different possible conclusions you could've taken from it, with each one pointing you in a different direction. Include one that positions the setback or obstacle in the overall arc of meeting your goal. Circle it.

I like to say, "No setback is permanent if you say it's not."

Write a few more statements like this that can help you reframe setbacks in the future.

....

....

....

....

....

....

....

....

> "In God's economy, nothing is ever wasted. Not your pain, nor your disappointments, not your setbacks. These are your tools. They can be used later as a recipe for your best work. Quit throwing the batter away."
>
> **—Bob**

FAILURES DON'T NAME YOU—GOD DOES

We're going to keep talking about failure because it's such a key part of chasing your dream, and I want you to really establish some new perspectives on it.

When you fail, what do you imagine God thinks?

....

....

. . . .

. . . .

. . . .

God isn't like a DMV examiner tapping His pencil on a scorecard scrutinizing your every move until you get it right. Remember His unconditional love? Remember what a big deal you are to Him? He has tremendous grace and kindness for you.

When you face your setbacks, a flood of lies will come at you—and fast. *I'm not good enough. I don't have what it takes to do this. What was I even thinking trying to accomplish this? I'll never get this done.*

You have to silence those lies, just like you silence limiting beliefs. Remember that some things we try will work; others won't. It's that simple. You have to learn what you can from the successes or setbacks and move on. Don't overidentify with either. Our failures don't name us—God does. If you're not hearing the name "beloved" whispered over your shoulder when you do a major faceplant or setback, it's not Jesus doing the talking.

What else do you think Jesus says to you when things don't work out? Who does He say you are?

....

....

....

....

....

....

....

....

....

....

....

....

....

Jesus will be with us while we navigate difficulties. We all screw up—often. Keep moving ahead. We need to keep our eyes on Jesus rather than caring how we look to everyone else. If we keep it about Him, we'll come to know more about Him while we're figuring out a few more things about ourselves.

What are some things you've learned about Jesus through past difficulties?

··

··

··

··

··

··

··

··

··

··

··

"Messing up doesn't mean *you* are a mess-up. It means you're a dreamer who's willing to take some risks, get a few scrapes, clear away the ashes, and build some new foundations."

—Bob

WEEK 42

KEEP YOUR EYE
ON THE PRIZE

When you are chasing an ambition, it can take you into uncharted territory. You might not know anyone who's attempted the thing you're trying to accomplish. If that's the case, you should take it as a signal that you're on the right track.

Take a few minutes and reconnect with your vision.

Write down in exquisite detail what will happen when you've made it a reality. Who will it help? What would an average Tuesday look and feel like when you're living out your dream?

....

....

....

....

....

....

....

....

....

....

....

....

....

....

....

....

I love to envision what it would be like when one of my ambitions explodes into the world, releasing love, hope, and inspiration into the lives of those around me. I get so excited by the possibilities. I get goose bumps and want to do a thousand push-ups and give high fives to everyone within a square mile. How about you?

WEEK 43

PACK YOUR EMERGENCY KIT

Faith and friendship are essential tools to keep us motivated when we face a major setback toward our dreams. Have an emergency kit of these ready when it happens to you. Do you have some favorite Bible verses God has used in your life to keep your head up? Is there a close friend or two who has a knack for encouraging you when times get tough?

Write those verses and those names here.

....

....

....

....

....

....

....

....

....

....

....

....

Here are a few more verses to add to your list:

- Be strong and do not give up. (2 Chronicles 15:7)
- Whatever you do, work at it with all your heart, as working for the Lord, not for human masters. (Colossians 3:23)
- Let us not become weary in doing good, for

at the proper time we will reap a harvest if we do not give up. (Galatians 6:9)

- If God is for us, who can be against us? . . . We are more than conquerors through him who loved us. (Romans 8:31, 37)
- I can do all this through him who gives me strength. (Philippians 4:13)

When you've hit a roadblock on your Dream Big journey, get those out. Read. Make the call. Don't be afraid to reach for some encouragement and truth exactly when you need it.

WEEK 44

DON'T YIELD TO DISAPPOINTMENT

When you face a setback, it's normal and natural to get into a funk. The problem comes when we stay there too long.

What's your tendency? Are you able to acknowledge a difficult spot you're in and find a way forward? Or does it become your new return address?

. . . .

. . . .

. . . .

. . . .

One way to steel yourself for the inevitable future setbacks you'll face is to take an inventory of how you've responded to setbacks in the past. It will give you some cheat notes on your own tendencies.

If you're a person who typically rams the roadblock, where have you drawn that strength from before?

. . . .

. . . .

. . . .

If you rolled over important relationships on the way toward your ambitions, what could you have done differently?

. . . .

. . . .

. . . .

If you tend to shrink back, where's that coming from?

....

....

....

....

....

....

....

....

....

Keep these notes handy, because eventually, you're going to need them.

One of my favorite ways to overcome a setback is to preplan what I'll do when it happens. We've done something like that earlier in this journal, but we're going to practice it again now.

Write out three specific things you'll do the next time you face a setback. Also describe how you'll find your grit while giving yourself grace. Keep in mind that whatever you choose to do to overcome a setback may not completely change your situation, but it will change you. And that's the starting point for moving forward.

....

....

....

....

....

....

Once you get your ambitions in your sights, no amount of failure has to keep you from trying again—as long as you don't yield to the disappointments. If you have clarity on what you want and why you want it, you'll have what it takes to make as many attempts as needed to get there.

> "Many of life's failures are people who did not realize how close they were to success when they gave up."
> **—Thomas Edison**

EXPECTANT WAITING

I'm an impatient guy. All my friends and family know this. As I've chased some of my dreams, though, I've experienced how patience is a powerful tool for the journey.

What about you?

....

....

Do you know your sweet spot between abdication and expectant waiting? Sometimes it's hard to recognize, but think about it.

What does purposeful waiting look like in your own life?

....

....

....

....

....

....

....

....

....

Fulfilling big dreams takes time. If it didn't, you'd have already fulfilled them. Rest in knowing you've planted seeds and done the work you needed to do to make something grow. Plus, remember, that thirty-eighth miracle could show up any minute. Keep a joyful sense of adventure and anticipation.

What would it look like for you to do that this week?

....

....

....

....

....

....

....

....

....

....

....

....

....

"The secret of waiting is the faith that the seed has been planted, that something has begun."
—Henri Nouwen

---✈

CHECK YOUR TIES

I've learned that pursuing your ambitions isn't a walk in the park; it's an assault on a tall mountain. Sometimes you'll find yourself hanging by crimped fingertips on the cliff face. When this happens, don't back off. This is normal. Just make sure you're securely "tied in" to a rock.

In the Bible, God is often described as a rock—someone immovable who we can always depend on. The people I've known who have tied their lives into

✈

Jesus didn't do it because they thought He'd keep them from falling; instead, they did it because they believed He could handle the weight of their failures when they did.

Think of someone who has stayed tied to Jesus as their rock, especially when they've faced difficulties. How did that affect their actions? What were the results?

....
....
....
....
....
....
....
....
....
....
....
....
....

If you want to stay after your ambitions, you need to stay tied to your rock. You'll need it if you're going to bear up under the weight of your setbacks. You also have to stay connected and open with the people around you. As we've said before, no one chasing a big ambition is going to get there on their own.

Are you securely tied in to your faith and relationships? Think hard about this. Can you really rely on them when you're dangling from a cliff face?

Get real with yourself and describe what things are like right now.

....

....

....

....

....

....

....

....

....

If you need to tighten some knots or click into some carabiners in your relationship with God, do it. If you need to reconnect more firmly with the people you depend on most, don't wait another second.

List three ways you can get more secure and do these things.

. . . .

. . . .

. . . .

. . . .

. . . .

. . . .

. . . .

. . . .

. . . .

. . . .

. . . .

. . . .

. . . .

LOOK HOW FAR YOU'VE COME

If you've been fully engaged in this process of discovery and self-reflection, my hunch is that you've covered quite a bit of distance so far.

Take a moment to reflect on where you started and where you are now. Do you have more clarity? More energy?

....

....

....

....

....

....

....

I know making your way through this journal is hard work, which is why you should stop right now and congratulate yourself for everything you've poured into this. Remember, you're worth it.

Take five minutes and write down what you're proud of in this process.

....

....

....

....

....

....

....

....

Are there any other small wins or half-steps forward to celebrate?

....
....
....
....
....
....
....
....
....
....
....
....
....
....
....

Go buy yourself a few medals or write yourself some notes of congratulation to open when you've made some progress.

SMALL THINGS LEAD TO BIG THINGS

One of the head-fakes we get as we pursue our most beautiful ambitions is thinking we have to go from step one to step twenty-three in one major leap. Don't fall for it. This isn't a sprint; this is a marathon God has invited you to run with Him.

Taking even a small action each day can lead to huge outcomes. When has that happened for you in the past? When did you consistently do little things that ultimately led to a significant experience?

Fill in the diagram below to get a visual of what happened.

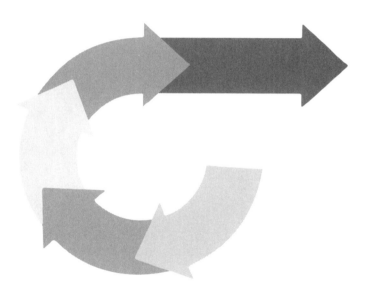

Revisit your lists from earlier in this journal—your list of dreams and the opportunities you're going to explore—and write down the ones that feel like small things that can lead to big things.

....

....

....

....

....

....

....

....

....

Star the one you'll do next. If you don't try, it won't happen. Give it a shot and see what opens up.

> "Great things do not just happen by impulse, but as a succession of small things linked together."
> **—Vincent van Gogh**

---▷

BE PICKY ABOUT
YOUR WORDS

Remember the story I told about rock climbing with my roommate Jack (*Dream Big*, chapter 27)? I thought I could hold his weight and belay him, but then I realized I hadn't secured our rope to a rock. The words I spoke to Jack to get him back to safety were incredibly important. I needed to be calm and truthful, not panicky and blabbering. I had to choose my words wisely.

---▷

You'll have to do the same as you're going after your ambitions. When you come across obstacles, don't default to hand-wringing, idle conversations laced with despair and disappointment. When you encounter difficult people, don't act like an umpire calling strikes and balls.

Be picky about your words. They have tremendous power. They might be the most powerful thing any of us have. Use them wisely and sparingly. Pick meaningful and lasting ones. Unlock their power with intention. Recognize that a few right words have the power to sustain you.

Here are three to start with: "Be not afraid."

Write out some things others have said to you that have inspired or helped you.

. . . .

. . . .

. . . .

. . . .

. . . .

. . . .

Write out some things you've said to others to encourage or strengthen them.

....
....
....
....
....
....
....
....

What other words of wisdom give you clarity?

....
....
....
....
....
....
....
....

WEEK 50

HOW TO LAND THE PLANE

As you've gone through this journal, you've been trying some new things. How has it gone?

In what ways have you gotten lift-off and made progress toward your ambitions?

. . . .

. . . .

. . . .

. . . .

Next, you need to focus on landing your ambitions like you would land a plane. Try following a process that pilots use: "pitch, pick, and point."

Pitching means you push the controls of the plane forward and *pitch* it toward the ground. You don't pull back or stall out when things get tough.

Then, you *pick* where you're going to land. I've felt the most disoriented when I haven't picked where I wanted to land next with my ambitions. You've got to have a clear target.

Last, you keep *pointing* at what you picked. It sounds simple enough, but in flying and in life, it's easy to get distracted and stop pointing at the right things. Rather than pointing at beautiful, truthful things, we sometimes point toward dark ones or ones that are merely entertaining. Paul talked about fixing our eyes on Jesus. Certainly do this and as you do, notice all the beautiful ambitions of yours that are adjacent to Him. If you don't, you could end up settling for things that merely work or are easily available and lose those things that are lasting and purposeful.

Make a plan now for how you're going to do this.

Pitch:

. . . .

. . . .

. . . .

. . . .

Pick:

. . . .

. . . .

. . . .

. . . .

Point:

. . . .

. . . .

. . . .

. . . .

Remember, pick something worth pointing all your energies at and don't take your eyes off of it. Keep pointing at it in the best or worst of circumstances. Do these things and you'll land your plane as you launch your ideas.

IT'S ALL WORTH IT

There's something safe and comforting about the planning process, isn't there? At some point, though, we just have to stop all the planning already. Book the flight. Buy the ring. Host the first meeting in your living room. Whatever it is, stop hovering ten feet above your dream. Pitch forward a little bit more and get your wheels on the ground.

As you do this, don't aim for perfection; look for proof that your ambition is taking shape in the world. Don't think it will all go smoothly. Be ready for the jolt when you touch down. Block out all the reasons this could go wrong or why you shouldn't try. Circle back to all of the insights and clarity you've gathered through this journal as your reminder that *your ambition is worth it. All of it*. It is worth everything you can throw at it. It's worth every sacrifice you'll make to turn your idea to reality.

Write out all the reasons why you're pursuing your beautiful ambition. How is it practicing for heaven? How will it affect others? What will it mean for you and your life?

....

....

....

....

....

....

....

....

....

STAY IN MOTION

Remember learning that thing in school where an object in motion tends to stay in motion and an object at rest tends to stay at rest? Much of this journal was designed to help you move from rest to motion. You've managed to get up in the plane. You've been soaring through the sky. Next, you're going to land the plane on this process. As you do, don't overlook the feeling of excitement and momentum you get from making some moves forward.

Now that you've reached the final week of this journal, you've identified a few dreams in your heart. You've taken action. You have a clear sense of what you'll do next and down the road. Look out to the life in front of you and take a deep breath. Tell yourself, "I am going to do this."

Write down this phrase for each one of your dreams: "I will [fill in the blank with your dream(s)]."

....

....

....

....

....

....

....

....

....

....

....

If you're willing to put in the work, you will find the life you've longed for. A life of purpose, full to the brim with intention and anticipation. A life lived with your eyes wide open, where you actually want what you see ahead of you rather than obsessing over the past or living scared about the future. A life that leads to purpose and legacy and fulfillment.

Describe how that would look for you and why you long for it.

. . . .

. . . .

. . . .

. . . .

. . . .

. . . .

. . . .

. . . .

. . . .

. . . .

. . . .

....
....
....
....
....
....
....
....
....
....

Somewhere out there, someone is praying that you'll put down your pen and spring into action. So get moving. Stay in motion. Keep at it. All of heaven is counting on you to show up and fully engage your beautiful life.

> "There is nothing like a dream
> to create the future."
> **—Victor Hugo**

BOOKS BY BOB GOFF
THAT WILL INSPIRE YOU!

Discover a secretly incredible
life in an ordinary world

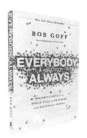

Become love in a world full of
setbacks and difficult people

365 days' worth of inspiring, unexpected,
humble teaching on grace and love that
will prepare you for the day ahead

Know what you want, why
you want it, and what you're
going to do about it

**Available wherever books, audio
books, and ebooks are sold**

NELSON
BOOKS

An Imprint of Thomas Nelson